20.90

DATE DUE

SEP 15 1999

EVERYDAY MATERIAL
SCIENCE EXPERIMENTS

PLASTICS & POLYMERS

Robert C. Mebane

Thomas R. Rybolt

Illustrations by Anni Matsick

TWENTY-FIRST CENTURY BOOKS

A Division of Henry Holt and Company
New York

Twenty-First Century Books
A Division of Henry Holt and Company, Inc.
115 West 18th Street
New York, NY 10011

Henry Holt® and colophon are trademarks of
Henry Holt and Company, Inc.
Publishers since 1866

Published in Canada by Fitzhenry & Whiteside Ltd.
195 Allstate Parkway, Markham, Ontario L3R 4T8

Library of Congress Cataloging-in-Publication Data

Mebane, Robert C.
Plastics and polymers / Robert C. Mebane and Thomas R. Rybolt;
illustrations by Anni Matsick.—1st ed.
p. cm. — (Everyday material science experiments)
Includes bibliographical references and index.
1. Polymers—Juvenile literature. 2. Plastics—Experiments—Juvenile
literature. [1. Plastics—Experiments. 2. Polymers—Experiments.]
I. Rybolt, Thomas R. II. Matsick, Anni, ill. III. Title. IV. Series:
Mebane, Robert C. Everyday material science experiments.
QD381.3.M43   1995
547.7—dc20   94–24963
                                                          CIP
                                                           AC

ISBN 0–8050–2843–9
First Edition 1995

Designed by Kelly Soong

Printed in Mexico
All first editions are printed on acid-free paper ∞.
10 9 8 7 6 5 4 3 2 1

For Dr. Michael Riemann, your influence never stops —R.M.

For my nephews, Bill Rencher and Dan Rencher   —T.R.

ACKNOWLEDGMENTS

We wish to thank Professor Mickey Sarquis of Miami University, Middletown, Ohio, for reading and making helpful comments on the manuscript and Dr. Tom Orofino of the University of Tennessee at Chattanooga, for his many helpful suggestions in the development of these experiments.

CONTENTS

INTRODUCTION 7

1 WATER-LOVING AND WATER-FEARING POLYMERS 9

2 SUPER ABSORBENT POLYMER 12

3 DIFFERENT TYPES OF POLYETHYLENE PLASTIC 14

4 FLOW LIKE A LIQUID AND BREAK LIKE A SOLID 17

5 NONSTICK POLYMER 20

6 SEEING COLORS IN PLASTIC WITH POLARIZED LIGHT 23

7 USING A POLYMER TO THICKEN A LIQUID 27

8 ODOR MOVING THROUGH A POLYMER 30

9 COMPARING THE HEAT INSULATION OF POLYMERS 33

10 HEATING AND COOLING WITH A BALLOON 36

11 MELTING PLASTICS 40

12 BREAKING DOWN A POLYMER 44

13 CHANGING THE SHAPE OF PLASTIC 47

14 A LONGER RUBBER BAND 50

15 BENDING COLD POLYMERS 54

16 BOUNCING BALLS 57

SCIENCE CONCEPTS 60

FURTHER READING 61

INDEX 62

INTRODUCTION

The world around you is filled with *Air and Other Gases, Water and Other Liquids, Salts and Solids, Metals,* and *Plastics and Polymers.* Some of these materials are part of our natural environment, and some are part of our created, industrial environment. The materials that we depend on for life and the materials that are part of our daily living all have distinct properties. These properties can be best understood through careful examination and experimentation.

Have you ever wondered why Teflon is slippery, how plastics are molded into shapes, how gravy thickens, or why some fabrics dry faster than others? In this book you will discover the answers to these and many other fascinating questions about *Plastics and Polymers.* In the process you will learn about plastics and polymers as materials—what they are made of, how they behave, and why they are important.

Each experiment is designed to stand alone. That is, it's not necessary to start with the first experiment and proceed to the second, then the third, and so on. Feel free to skip around—that's part of the fun of discovery. As you do the experiments, think about the results and what they mean to you. Also, think about how the results apply to the world around you.

At the beginning of each experiment, you will find one or more icons identifying the important physical science concepts dealt with in the experiment. For example, if the icon ✳ appears at the top of the page, it means that matter, one of the basic concepts of science, will be explored. On page 60 you will find a listing of all the icons—matter, energy, light, and heat—and the experiments to which they relate.

As you carry out the experiments in this book, be sure to follow carefully any special safety instructions that are given. **For some experiments, a ⬣ means that you should have an adult work with you**. For all your experiments, you need to make sure that an adult knows what you are doing. Remember to clean up after your experiment is completed.

1

WATER-LOVING AND WATER-FEARING POLYMERS

MATTER

MATERIALS NEEDED

Cloth of 100 percent
cotton

Cloth of 100 percent
polyester

Felt pen

Two small plates

Measuring spoon

Water

Did you know that some types of fabric dry faster than others? In this experiment you will learn why.

For this experiment you will need two pieces of fabric, one that is 100 percent cotton and one that is 100 percent polyester. Cloth scraps could be used for this experiment. Each piece of cloth should be about 10 in. by 5 in. (25 cm by 13 cm). In addition they should be similar in texture (look and feel about the same). If you do not have scrap cloth that you can use for this experiment, both types of fabric can be purchased at fabric stores and many large department stores.

To label the two pieces of cloth, use a felt pen to write the letter *C* in a corner of the cotton cloth and the letter *P* in a corner of the polyester cloth. Fold each piece of cloth in half lengthwise, and place the folded pieces of cloth on separate small plates. Set the small plates on a table where they will not be disturbed.

Pour 1 teaspoon (5 ml) of water onto each piece of cloth, as shown in Figure A. Pick up and feel each piece after the water has completely soaked into the fabric and then place the pieces back

FIGURE A

on the small plates. Feel the two pieces of cloth again after 1 hour. Do they both still feel damp? Repeat your testing for dampness every hour for several hours.

After a couple of hours, you should find that the polyester cloth feels dry while the cotton cloth still feels damp. Cloth made of polyester dries faster than cloth made of cotton.

Both cotton and polyester are polymers. Natural fibers such as cotton and linen are considered natural polymers because they consist mostly of cellulose, the major structural part of woody plants. Cotton is made by plants linking thousands of glucose molecules in long chains. Glucose is a simple sugar made by plants during photosynthesis.

Cellulose is a hydrophilic polymer. *Hydrophilic* means "water-loving." Cellulose is hydrophilic because the glucose molecules that make it up are polar. Water is polar, and polar substances are attracted to each other.

There are many different types of polyester polymers. The

most widely used polyester is Dacron. Dacron is used to make fibers for cloth. Dacron is made from chemical substances obtained from petroleum.

Dacron and other polyester molecules do not attract water. Substances that do not attract water are called *hydrophobic*, which means "water-fearing." Polyester molecules are nonpolar. Nonpolar molecules and polar molecules do not strongly attract each other.

The water on the polyester fiber evaporates quickly because the water is not held strongly to the fiber. The cotton cloth dried more slowly because the water is held more strongly by the cotton fibers.

Special fabrics have been developed recently specifically for people who enjoy outdoor activities such as running, skiing, and hiking. These special fabrics are made from polymers, mostly polyester, that are hydrophobic. Clothing made from these special fabrics does not retain water and dries very quickly. Some examples are Thermax, Thermastat, Polypro, Capilene, and Coolmax. Can you think of other uses for hydrophobic fabrics?

2

SUPER ABSORBENT POLYMER

MATTER

MATERIALS NEEDED

Disposable diaper
(with "ultra" indicated
on label)

Measuring cup

Plastic cup

Water

Spoon

Super absorbent polymer is a special type of material that is used to help absorb liquid. In this experiment you will explore what happens when water is added to super absorbent polymer.

Tear open a disposable diaper (use one of the brands that have the word "ultra" on the package), and remove some of the white cellulose filling that looks like cotton. Cellulose is a natural substance found in the woody part of plants. This filling should contain small particles of super absorbent polymer. You will not see these particles because they are mixed with the cellulose filling, which is made from cotton fibers or refined wood pulp.

Put ½ cup (120 ml) of this filling material in a large plastic cup. Then add 1 cup (0.24 l) of water to the plastic cup. Using a spoon, stir together this mixture of water, cellulose filling, and super absorbent polymer, as shown in Figure A. Wait about 1 minute, and stir again.

Wait about 4 minutes, and then turn the cup on its side. Does any of the water come out of the cup? Has the water in the cup changed its appearance? How does the water in the cup look?

FIGURE A

You will probably find that the water in the cup has changed to a solid that looks and moves like jelly.

You may want to see how much more water you can add and still form a solid gelatinlike substance. Try adding another ½ cup (120 ml) of water to the mixture in the cup and stir. Wait 5 minutes. Repeat this procedure until a solid no longer forms. Then try adding another ½ cup of diaper filling, stir, and see if the mixture will once again form a gelatinlike solid.

Super absorbent polymer is added to thin disposable diapers to help absorb liquid. A natural polymer like cellulose absorbs some water, but super absorbent polymer absorbs up to 40 times its own weight in water. When you formed a solid mass with 1 cup of water and ½ cup of diaper filling, only a small amount of super absorbent polymer was present.

Super absorbent polymer is made of molecules that can move apart and trap water molecules. The polymer molecules are linked together like a tangled mass of spaghetti. Imagine beads entering this tangled mass and the spaghetti strands spreading apart and trapping the beads. Super absorbent polymer is like the spaghetti, and the beads are like molecules of water.

3

DIFFERENT TYPES OF POLYETHYLENE PLASTIC

MATERIALS NEEDED

Plastic lid or other
   piece of plastic with
   the code *4, LDPE*

Scissors

Ruler

Milk jug or other
   piece of plastic with
   the code *2, HDPE*

In this experiment you will examine some of the differences between two forms of the same polymer—high-density and low-density polyethylene.

Find a plastic lid or other piece of plastic that has the letters *LDPE* and the code number *4* inside a triangle. Make sure you use a piece of plastic with this code on it. This code indicates that the plastic is made of low-density polyethylene. Cut a 2-in. (5-cm) square out of this plastic. Make sure to include the LDPE code as part of the square.

Find a milk jug or other piece of plastic that has the letters *HDPE* and a code number 2 inside a triangle. Make sure you use a piece of plastic with this code on it. This code indicates that the plastic is made of high-density polyethylene. Cut a 2-in. (5-cm) square out of this plastic.

The two squares of plastic should be about the same thickness—0.04 in. (about 1 mm) or less. Rub your finger across each piece of plastic. Do they feel different?

Make a cut 0.3 in. (0.75 cm) deep on one side of both

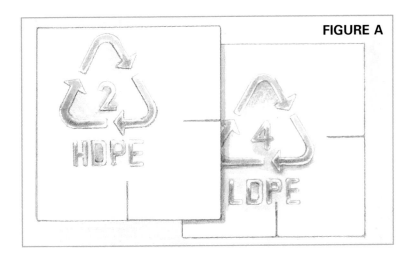

squares of plastic. Make a second cut on each plastic square on a side next to the first cut, as shown in Figure A.

Hold the square of LDPE on each side of one of the cuts and try to tear the plastic. Try to tear the other cut on the LDPE. Now try to tear each of the cuts on the square of HDPE. Is one piece of plastic harder to tear than the other?

You probably found the LDPE easier to cut with scissors than the HDPE. You may be able to feel a difference between the two types of plastic. The LDPE will feel waxy and slightly slippery to the touch. The HDPE is dry and not waxy or slippery. You may also find that the high-density polyethylene is stiffer and harder to bend than the low-density polyethylene.

You probably found the HDPE square much harder to tear than the LDPE. You probably could not tear the HDPE. The LDPE may be harder to tear in one direction than another, but you should be able to easily tear at least one of the cuts on the LDPE.

Polyethylene is widely used for plastic bags, wrappings, and containers. Billions of pounds of low-density and high-density polyethylene are made every year. Polyethylene is made by chemically linking together, like paper clips in a long chain, thousands of small ethylene molecules. In this model, each paper clip would represent 1 ethylene unit. The final chain would represent the long polyethylene molecule. However, high- and low-density polyethylenes differ in the way the chain ethylene units are arranged. HDPE consists of more straight chain regions, whereas LDPE is more highly branched, with shorter side chains. As a result, LDPE does not pack together as tightly as does HDPE and thus has a lower density and is easier to cut or tear.

Polymerization is the process by which a polymer is formed. Low-density polyethylene is made by polymerization of ethylene at pressures up to 3,000 times as great as the pressure of the air in our atmosphere. High-density polyethylene is made by the polymerization of ethylene with a special metal catalyst (a catalyst is a substance used to speed up a chemical reaction) at much lower pressures than LDPE.

The regions of the polyethylene molecules that are lined up next to each other are called *crystalline regions*. Regions of the molecules that do not line up are called *amorphous regions*. The molecules are held more strongly together in crystalline regions than they are in amorphous regions. HDPE consists of mostly long, straight chain regions that can fold neatly together to make many crystalline regions. These crystalline regions make HDPE a stiff and strong polymer that is difficult to cut or tear and well suited for bottles that must hold a liquid without breaking.

LDPE consists of highly branched chains that cannot fit neatly together. These short chain branches are amorphous regions that make the polymer more flexible. Such a polymer is easier to cut or tear because the molecules are not neatly folded together but randomly intermingled, like branches from nearby trees. Low-density polyethylene is used to make thin films for wrapping foods to keep them fresh.

The chemicals that make up a polymer, as well as the exact arrangement of the polymer chains, determine many important polymer properties. Can you explain why HDPE has a greater density (the same volume is heavier) than LDPE? Can you explain why LDPE feels slippery and HDPE does not?

4

FLOW LIKE A LIQUID AND BREAK LIKE A SOLID

MATTER

MATERIALS NEEDED

Silly Putty (available
 in most toy stores)

Ruler

Did you know that certain materials can behave as either solids or liquids? In this experiment you will show that a polymer can act as both a solid and a liquid.

To begin the experiment, roll the Silly Putty between your hands until you form a cylinder about 2 in. (5 cm) long. While holding the two ends of the cylinder, one in each hand, slowly pull on the Silly Putty. Continue to pull until you can no longer move your hands farther apart. Roll the Silly Putty into a cylinder again and repeat the experiment.

Roll the Silly Putty back into a cylinder, this time about 4 in. (10 cm) long. With one hand, hold the cylinder at the top straight up and down. With your other hand, hold a ruler next to the cylinder, as shown in Figure A. Continue to hold the cylinder of Silly Putty next to the ruler for 30 seconds to 1 minute. Does the cylinder get longer as you hold it straight up and down?

Again, roll the Silly Putty into a cylinder about 2 in. (5 cm) long. Firmly grasp the center of the cylinder with both hands. Your thumbs and index fingers should be touching. Quickly and firmly, pull on the Silly Putty. What happens? Repeat this part of the experiment as many times as you like.

You should notice that as you slowly pull on the Silly Putty

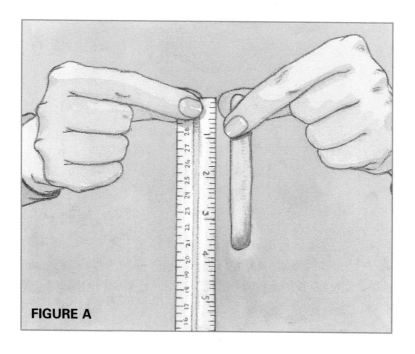

FIGURE A

with both hands, a thin string of Silly Putty forms. You may also observe that this thin string, if it does not break first, continually sags, or moves toward the floor. When you hold a cylinder of Silly Putty straight up and down next to a ruler, you should actually see the cylinder of Silly Putty get longer and longer as gravity pulls it to the floor. In these two experiments, the Silly Putty is behaving like a thick, gooey liquid.

On the other hand, when you hold the Silly Putty firmly and pull on it quickly with both hands, you should observe that it breaks sharply, as if it were a solid.

To understand how Silly Putty can behave as a liquid or a solid, we first need to learn about the polymer found in Silly Putty. Silly Putty is an example of a *silicone polymer.* Silicone polymers consist of long chains containing silicon, oxygen, carbon, and hydrogen. If you could see a portion of a silicone polymer molecule, it would appear as a straight chain of alternating silicon and oxygen atoms, similar to a necklace containing two different alternating beads. Attached to the silicon atoms of the polymer chain are groups made of carbon and hydrogen atoms.

Your piece of Silly Putty contains numerous individual silicone polymer chains that are coiled and intertwined. When you slowly pull on the Silly Putty, the individual polymer chains have enough time to slide over each other, and the material behaves as a thick liquid. On the other hand, when you pull sharply on the Silly Putty, the individual polymer chains are not able to slide over each other easily because of friction between the polymer chains. In this case the Silly Putty breaks as if it were a solid.

Can you think of some practical uses for a polymer that behaves as both a liquid and a solid?

There are many other materials in addition to silicone polymers that can behave as either liquids or solids, depending upon the way they are pulled. Some common examples are chewing gum, taffy candy, and asphalt.

5

NONSTICK POLYMER

MATTER

HEAT

MATERIALS NEEDED

Egg

Bowl

Fork

Teflon-coated frying pan (nonstick frying pan)

Regular metal frying pan

Stove

Tablespoon

Spatula

Plate

❗ **Alert! Adult supervision needed.**

In this experiment you will study a unique property of the polymer known as Teflon. To begin the experiment, crack open an egg and add its contents to a bowl. Beat the egg with a fork until it is mixed well (about 30 seconds).

Place each frying pan on a heating element on the stove. Add 1 tablespoon (15 ml) of the beaten egg to each pan. Turn on the heating elements under the two frying pans, and heat each pan over medium heat. Continue to heat the eggs until they are completely cooked. The eggs will be firm and not runny when they are completely cooked. Make sure you turn the stove off when you are through cooking. Use a spatula to remove the cooked eggs from the frying pans. Be careful not to touch the hot pans. Place the eggs on a plate. What differences do you observe?

You should find it much easier to remove the cooked egg

from the Teflon-coated frying pan than from the regular metal frying pan. In fact, if your Teflon-coated pan is fairly new, you may find that the cooked egg does not stick to the pan at all, but actually slides around. In contrast, you may find that the cooked egg sticks firmly to the regular frying pan.

Invented by E. I. Du Pont de Nemours & Co. in 1938, Teflon is the trade name for the polymer known as *polytetrafluoroethylene* (PTFE). It is similar to the polymer *polyethylene* (PE). Polyethylene is used to make plastic storage bags, trash bags, milk containers, and other useful plastic items.

Both Teflon and polyethylene molecules consist of long chains of carbon atoms. Attached to each carbon atom in polyethylene are hydrogen atoms and other carbon atoms. Teflon molecules differ from polyethylene molecules in that fluorine atoms, instead of hydrogen atoms, are attached to the long chains of carbon atoms, as shown in Figure A.

The long chains of carbon atoms in Teflon are twisted in a spiral arrangement much like a spiral telephone cord. The fluorine atoms stick out from the twisted spiral of carbon atoms. This

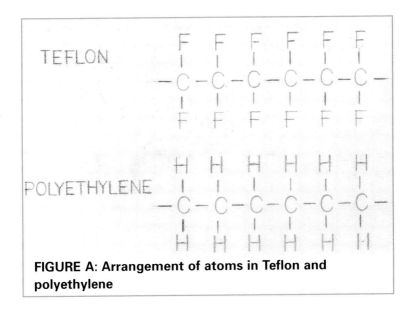

FIGURE A: Arrangement of atoms in Teflon and polyethylene

arrangement of the fluorine atoms, along with the fact that the bond between a carbon atom and a fluorine atom is very strong and difficult to break, is responsible for the unique properties of this important polymer.

One unique and important property of Teflon is that it is very slippery. As a result, it is difficult for materials such as food to stick to Teflon. Teflon is slippery because there is very little attraction between the Teflon molecules on the surface of the pan and the molecules of the material placed on the Teflon surface.

In this experiment the egg sticks to the frying pan not coated with Teflon because there is a strong attraction between the surface of the metal frying pan and the egg. Normally, when food is cooked in a frying pan not coated with Teflon, cooking oil or butter is added to the pan to keep the food from sticking. The cooking oil forms a barrier between the food and the metal pan.

Teflon has other unique properties. For example, unlike most plastics, Teflon is nonflammable and does not break down at high temperatures. It can be used at temperatures up to 500°F (260°C)—the highest temperature most cooking ovens reach.

Teflon does not react with most chemicals, so it is often used to make materials that will be constantly exposed to harsh chemicals such as acids and bases. It is highly weather-resistant and is not changed by sunlight. Sheets of Teflon-coated fabric are sometimes used as roof coverings. Can you think of future uses for Teflon or other nonstick polymers?

6

SEEING COLORS IN PLASTIC WITH POLARIZED LIGHT

MATERIALS NEEDED

Two pairs of polarized sunglasses

Lamp

Plastic sandwich bag

In this experiment you will use polarized sunglasses to learn something about the arrangement of long polymer molecules in a plastic sandwich bag.

To begin the experiment, you must make sure you have polarized sunglasses. To test for polarization, take the two pairs of sunglasses and hold the right lens of one of the pairs in front of the right lens of the other pair. Look through the two lenses at a lamp that is switched on. While keeping the lenses parallel to each other, slowly rotate one of them while holding the other one still. If both pairs of sunglasses are polarized, you should see the lamp change from light to dark.

Polarized light consists of light rays that are all oriented in the same direction. Light rays in ordinary light are oriented randomly and in all directions. When ordinary light strikes a polarized lens, only those rays oriented in one direction (up and down) are allowed to pass through.

Now hold the right lens of one pair of sunglasses behind a plastic sandwich bag, as shown in Figure A, and hold the right lens of the other pair of glasses in front of the plastic bag. You may want to ask a friend to hold the plastic bag while you hold the sunglasses. While looking at a lamp through both pairs of sun-

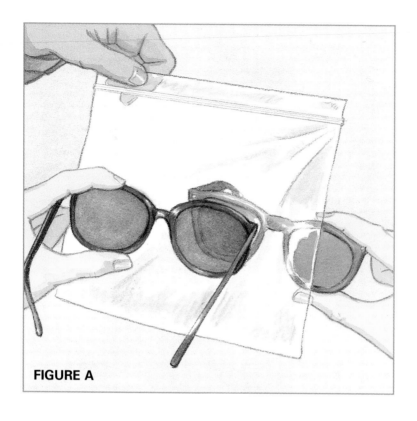

FIGURE A

glasses and the plastic sandwich bag, rotate the pair of sunglasses that is in front of the sandwich bag. What do you observe?

While holding one of the edges of the plastic bag with both hands close together, pull on the plastic bag until the plastic stretches less than 0.5 in. (1.3 cm). Now hold the right lens of one pair of sunglasses behind the stretched portion of the plastic bag, and hold the right lens of the other pair of sunglasses in front of the same section. Rotate the pair that is in front of the plastic. What do you observe?

You should observe that when you hold the plastic sandwich bag between the two pairs of sunglasses and rotate the front pair of sunglasses, the light coming through the sunglasses still changes from light to dark just as it did when the plastic sandwich bag was not between the two pairs of sunglasses. However, when you repeated the experiment, you should see different colors in the plastic as you rotated one of the pairs of sunglasses.

More than likely, the plastic sandwich bag you used for this experiment is made of the polymer called polyethylene. Polyethylene molecules can be extremely large and are made by linking into long chains smaller molecules called *ethylene molecules*. The plastic bag contains numerous polyethylene molecules. The long chains of polyethylene molecules in the bag randomly fold and twist around one another.

Before you stretched the plastic bag, the polyethylene molecules in the bag were randomly coiled and twisted around one another in no particular order. This is known as the *relaxed state* of the polymer molecules. Polarized light passes unchanged through plastic that contains polymer molecules in a relaxed state. This is why the light coming through the polarized sunglasses appeared the same whether the plastic bag was held between the two pairs of sunglasses or not.

But when you stretched the plastic bag, some of the randomly coiled and twisted polyethylene molecules in the bag became straightened and aligned next to each other, as shown in Figure B. When the long polymer molecules are straightened, they are no longer random, but are said to be *ordered*.

Polarized light can change when it passes through a group of molecules that are all aligned in a particular direction. This is what you observe in this experiment. The polarized light coming through the pair of sunglasses held behind the plastic bag changes direction slightly as it passes through the spot in the plastic bag that was stretched. This spot contains straightened and aligned chains of polyethylene molecules. You can tell the polarized light is changed as it passes through the stretched piece of plastic by the colors that are produced as you rotate the front pair of sunglasses.

Repeat this experiment with other objects made of plastic, such as a clear, flexible cup or drink bottle or the plastic ring that holds the cans in a six-pack of beverages. Is polarized light

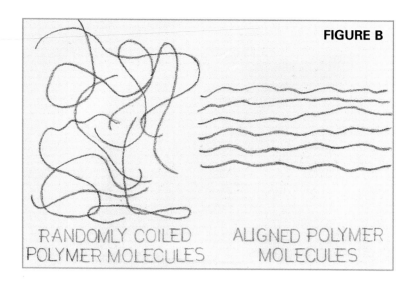

FIGURE B

RANDOMLY COILED
POLYMER MOLECULES

ALIGNED POLYMER
MOLECULES

changed as it passes through these pieces of plastic? If the polarized light is unaffected, the polymer molecules in the plastic are not oriented.

Before building a complex object, engineers will often build a small-scale model of the complex object out of plastic. They use the plastic model to understand how a particular force, such as a weight, may cause stress in the object. The engineers use polarized light to look for colors and patterns in the plastic model when a force or weight is placed on the object. Can you think of other uses?

7

USING A POLYMER TO THICKEN A LIQUID

| LIGHT | MATTER |

MATERIALS NEEDED

Measuring cup and
  spoons

Water

Saucepan

Stove

Small jar with a tight-
  fitting lid

Flour

Spoon for stirring

❗ **Alert! Adult supervision needed.**

In this experiment you will explore the effects of a polymer present in flour on hot and cold water.

To start the experiment, place 1 cup (0.24 l) of water into a saucepan and heat it on a stove. While the water is heating, pour ¼ cup (60 ml) of cold water into a jar with a tight-fitting lid. Then add 3 tablespoons (45 ml) of flour to the jar, secure the lid, and shake vigorously for 15 seconds. Describe the appearance of the flour-and-water mixture.

When the water in the saucepan starts to boil, turn off the heat. Give the jar containing the flour and cold water a good shake. Remove the lid from the jar, and continually stir the hot water in the saucepan with a spoon as you *slowly* pour the cold flour-and-water mixture into the saucepan, as shown in Figure A. Turn on the stove again and heat the saucepan over medium-low heat for 2 minutes, continually stirring the contents of the saucepan during heating. Then turn the stove off.

FIGURE A

You should observe that when you first add the cold flour-and-water mixture to the hot water, the hot water gets cloudy, but not thick. However, after stirring for a few seconds, you should notice that the hot water starts to clear and becomes thicker. To understand how the mixture becomes thick, we first need to learn about flour and how it can change in hot water.

Wheat flour is a complex mixture, but it consists mostly of starch. Made by plants, starch is a polymer containing thousands of sugar molecules linked together. The sugar molecule found in starch is called *glucose*. Glucose is made by plants during *photosynthesis*, a process by which plants convert some of the energy of the sun into food. Starch is an important energy source for plants and for animals that eat plants.

Plants also make a polymer called *cellulose*, which contains thousands of glucose units linked together. Cellulose is the major structural part of woody plants and natural fibers such as cotton and linen. Cellulose and starch differ in the way their glucose units are linked together. Can you think of reasons why plants might make two different polymers from glucose?

Plants store starch molecules in tiny sacs called *granules*. A single granule contains many long starch molecules. These molecules are coiled and intertwined, causing them to stick tightly together. The clumped molecules do not allow light to pass directly through the granules. Instead, light is deflected, and this is why flour looks like a white powder rather than like clear granules.

Normally it is not easy for water to get inside starch granules. However, when starch granules are mixed with hot water, the hot water enters the granules and causes them to swell, like raisins left in water for several hours. As the granules swell with water, they move more slowly and actually get in one another's way. This slowness of movement of the swollen starch granules makes the mixture thick. Interestingly, a starch granule can absorb an amount of water equal to 25 times its own weight.

Once inside the granule, the hot water forces the tightly packed starch molecules to move apart. When they move apart, they become surrounded by water molecules instead of other starch molecules. When the individual starch molecules become separated from one another by the water, light can pass more easily through the granules; and this is why the flour-and-water mixture becomes clear soon after it is heated and stirred.

This experiment is basically a recipe for making a sauce, or gravy. Cooks have known for a long time that flour and other starches, such as cornstarch, can be used to thicken a liquid.

Latex house paint is made in a similar way. A polymer called a *latex polymer* is added to water to give it just the right thickness. *Pigments*, or coloring agents, are then added to the mixture, along with certain other substances, to create the paint.

8

ODOR MOVING THROUGH A POLYMER

MATTER

MATERIALS NEEDED

Ziploc plastic bag (any size)

Peppermint extract (You can use other extracts as well, such as vanilla or almond. Aftershave or perfume also works in this experiment.)

Plate

Have you ever had to add air to a basketball, soccer ball, or tire? Have you ever wondered why air must be added occasionally to these inflatable objects? In this experiment you will explore why.

To begin the experiment, smell the outside of an unused Ziploc bag. Then open the bag, and put your hands inside it to open it as fully as possible. Now carefully put 2 or 3 drops of peppermint extract (or any of the other scented liquids listed in materials, above) inside the bag, as shown in Figure A. Make sure no extract drips on the outside of the bag. As you seal the bag, try to keep as much air inside it as you can. Shake the bag for a few seconds, and then smell the outside of the bag. Place the bag on a plate, set the plate on a table, and leave it there for 30 minutes. After this time, pick up the bag and smell the outside of the bag again.

You should find that the outside of an unused Ziploc bag has little or no odor. However, you should be able to smell pepper-

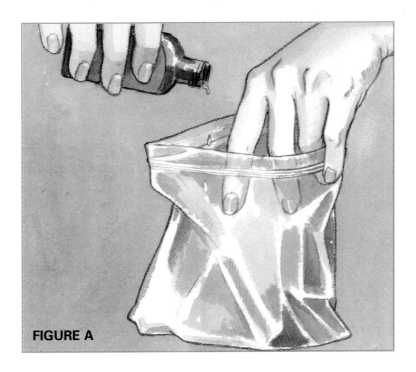

FIGURE A

mint on the outside of the bag after you have added peppermint extract and sealed the bag with air inside. Do you know why?

Most plastic Ziploc-type bags (and garbage bags) are made from polyethylene. Polyethylene is a polymer made by linking into long chains smaller molecules called ethylene molecules. The most common way to make a film of polyethylene suitable for storage bags and trash bags is to heat bulk polyethylene to 446°F (230°C) to make the polymer very soft. Then the soft polyethylene is forced through a thin slit, usually with a gas, to form a continuous thin film of polyethylene, which is cut and made into the final product.

Polyethylene is the ideal material for making plastic bags and bottles because it is waterproof, mostly clear in appearance, and nontoxic. In addition, it is a relatively inexpensive and tough material that resists tearing.

There are many individual polyethylene molecules in a plastic bag. If you could actually see them, they would appear like the branches of a tree. There are many overlapping layers of branched polyethylene molecules in the thin film that forms the bag, but there are still tiny openings, or pores, in the plastic bag. These tiny openings are large enough to allow small molecules, like those in air and peppermint molecules, to pass through the plastic bag. This is why you can smell peppermint on the outside of the Ziploc bag even though you sealed all the peppermint inside the bag.

The extent to which a substance will allow gas (or liquid) to move through it is called its *permeability*. The rubber polymer used to make basketballs, soccer balls, and bicycle tires is highly permeable to air. This is why you occasionally have to add air to these inflated objects. Some polymers have extremely low permeabilities to gases such as air. Examples include the plastic film used in certain potato chip bags and the plastic film used to make certain helium-filled balloons that stay inflated for long periods of time.

9

COMPARING THE HEAT INSULATION OF POLYMERS

ENERGY

HEAT

MATERIALS NEEDED

Regular polystyrene
cup

Styrofoam cup

Ice cubes

Clock or watch

Can two cups made of the same polymer differ in how well they insulate or keep things cold? In this experiment you will compare the flow of heat through two different forms of a polymer called *polystyrene*.

You need two drinking cups that are close to the same size. One cup should be made of regular polystyrene plastic. Codes identifying the type of plastic used are usually molded into the bottom of containers or cups. Regular polystyrene plastic is indicated by the code number 6 inside a triangle and the letters *PS* beneath the triangle. The cup may be clear or colored. The other cup should be made of styrofoam, another form of polystyrene. You can recognize a styrofoam cup because it is white, lightweight, and soft. You can easily make a mark on it with your fingernail. This type of cup is often used for hot drinks such as coffee.

Fill both cups with the same amount of ice. Feel the outside of each cup. Do they feel warm or cold to the touch? Wait about 15 minutes, and feel each cup again. Is the outside of the regular polystyrene cup cold? Is the outside of the styrofoam cup cold? Wait 15 more minutes, and check both cups again.

You will probably find that the outside of the regular polystyrene cup gets colder than the outside of the styrofoam cup. Styrofoam can insulate, or prevent heat from passing through the cup. As heat leaves the cup and flows into the melting ice, the cup becomes colder. Heat flows through the polystyrene cup much quicker than it does through the styrofoam cup.

Polystyrene is made by linking together a number of styrene molecules. Polystyrene was first sold in the 1930s by a German company, I. G. Farbenindustrie. Today, around the world, billions of pounds of polystyrene are made every year. One of the common uses of polystyrene is to make disposable plates, cups, and utensils.

Styrofoam is an expanded form of polystyrene that was first introduced by the Dow Chemical Company in the United States. Styrofoam is used to insulate drinking cups and ice chests as well as the walls of buildings, railroad cars, and trucks.

One way to make styrofoam is to use polystyrene beads that contain *pentane*. When the beads are heated in a *mold* (an empty metal container), the heat causes the pentane to change from a liquid to a gas. As the gas forms, the polystyrene beads swell and the polymer expands to form a lightweight material. As the beads swell, they stick together and form an object in the shape of the mold. If you look closely at a styrofoam cup, you will see it is made of many tiny pieces stuck together like a jigsaw puzzle.

Making styrofoam is somewhat like popping popcorn. When popcorn is heated, water trapped in the center of each popcorn kernel changes from a liquid to a gas. As the gas forms, it spreads apart soft starch material and the kernel puffs out. Compare the size of an unpopped kernel of corn to a popped one. Do you see how small polystyrene beads could spread apart into softer, lighter styrofoam?

In your experiment, the styrofoam cup is about the same weight as the regular polystyrene cup, but the styrofoam cup is much thicker. Why do you think the styrofoam cup is thicker than the regular polystyrene cup?

Heat cannot move through a gas as easily as it can through a solid, so gas is a good insulator. For example, there is a special kind of window that uses two *panes* (pieces of glass) with air trapped between them. This double-pane window is often used in cold regions because it insulates better than a window made of a single pane of glass. The gas trapped in styrofoam makes it more difficult for heat to move through styrofoam than through regular polystyrene.

Heat easily passes through the regular polystyrene cup, and so the outside of the cup gets cold. Heat passes slowly through the styrofoam cup, so the outside of the styrofoam cup does not get cold. Do you think ice will melt quicker in the regular polystyrene cup or the styrofoam cup? Can you design an experiment to test your hypothesis and measure any differences you observe?

HEATING AND COOLING WITH A BALLOON

ENERGY   HEAT

MATERIAL NEEDED
Balloon

In this experiment you will learn about energy changes by stretching and unstretching a balloon.

To begin, hold an unstretched balloon to your lower lip for a few seconds to feel its temperature. You can also touch the unstretched balloon to your forehead because your forehead, like your lips, is sensitive to changes in temperature. While holding the balloon, as shown in Figure A, quickly stretch it and immediately touch the tight, stretched balloon to your lower lip (or forehead). Does the balloon feel warm? Where does this heat come from?

Before we try to understand where the heat in the stretched balloon comes from, let's think about what is done to the balloon in this experiment. First, we must realize that an unstretched balloon does not become stretched all by itself. Instead, work must be done on the balloon to stretch it.

Work is what is necessary to cause a change in something that normally will not change by itself. For example, water flows downhill, not uphill. To get water uphill, work must be done by a pump or by a person simply carrying the water up the hill in a bucket. In the same sense, work must be done on a balloon to stretch it. When you stretch a balloon, you are doing work on it.

Work requires energy. Common forms of energy include

36

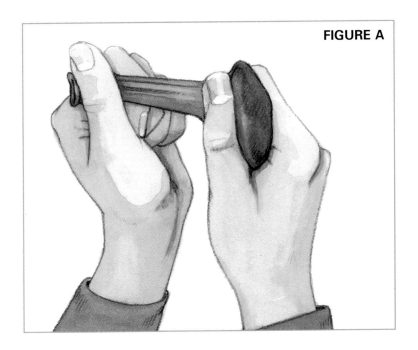

heat, light, sound, mechanical energy, electrical energy, and chemical energy. Different forms of energy can be interchanged. For example, electrical energy can be changed into sound energy with a speaker, and it is transformed into light and heat energy in an incandescent lamp. When gasoline is burned in the engine of a car, chemical energy is changed into heat and mechanical energy, which allows the car to move.

Let's return now to the question of where the heat comes from when the balloon is stretched. To stretch a balloon, you must move your hands apart while holding it. In other words, you must do work on it. The energy required to move your hands apart comes from your arm muscles and is a type of mechanical energy. When the balloon is stretched, some of the mechanical energy supplied by your arm muscles is transformed into heat. You feel this heat as a rise in the temperature of the stretched balloon.

Your muscles obtain energy to do work from the food you eat. The form of energy in food is chemical energy. Your muscles convert the chemical energy in food into mechanical energy for doing work.

Green plants are the source for all the food available on earth. When you eat fruits and vegetables, you obtain chemical energy directly from green plants. When you eat meat or dairy products, you still obtain chemical energy from green plants, but indirectly. For example, the milk in an ice-cream bar is food made by a cow. The cow makes the milk from green plants. This energy sequence is called a *food chain*.

The chemical energy stored in green plants is made by a complex process called photosynthesis. Through photosynthesis, green plants convert energy from the sun (*solar energy*) into chemical energy that is stored as food. With this knowledge, we can now say that the heat that formed in the stretched balloon actually came from the sun through a series of energy changes. Figure B traces these energy changes.

Now try this experiment. Stretch a balloon tightly and leave it stretched for 10 seconds. Then quickly bring your hands together to unstretch the balloon. Touch this unstretched balloon

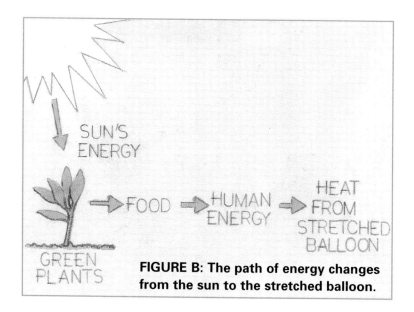

SUN'S ENERGY

GREEN PLANTS →FOOD →HUMAN ENERGY →HEAT FROM STRETCHED BALLOON

FIGURE B: The path of energy changes from the sun to the stretched balloon.

to your lower lip. The balloon should feel cool. In fact, you may notice that it feels cooler than an unstretched balloon. How does the balloon become cooler than before the balloon was stretched?

As mentioned before, when you stretch the balloon, you do work on the balloon. Some of the energy associated with this work is converted into heat. When the stretched balloon is allowed to relax, some of the energy in the balloon is changed into work and the temperature of the balloon decreases.

To conclude, you have learned that a balloon can be used to heat or cool. You have also learned that work is needed to make the balloon heat or cool. In addition, you have learned that energy can be converted from one form to another.

MELTING PLASTICS

HEAT

MATTER

MATERIALS NEEDED

Milk jug or other
  piece of plastic with
  the code *2, HDPE*

Scissors

Ruler

Four flat plastic
  buttons

Aluminum pie pan

Oven

Clock or watch

Oven mitt

! **Alert! Adult supervision needed.**

Do plastics melt if heated? In this experiment you will see what happens to two different types of plastics at high temperatures.

You will need a milk jug or other piece of plastic that has the letters *HDPE* beneath a triangle with the code number 2 inside it. A code number and letters are usually molded into the bottom of plastic containers. The code identifies the plastic as high-density polyethylene.

Cut out four pieces of the plastic, each about 0.4 in. (1 cm) wide and about 1.5 in. (4 cm) long. Fold each piece into thirds to make a triangle. Set these triangular pieces of HDPE and the plastic buttons on an aluminum pie pan, as shown in Figure A.

Turn the oven temperature to 400°F (204°C), and wait 20 minutes until the oven is hot. Use an oven mitt to place the aluminum pie pan on a rack in the oven. Close the oven door and

FIGURE A

wait 10 minutes while the plastic samples become hot. **Do not heat longer than 10 minutes.**

Turn off the oven, and use the oven mitt to carefully remove the pie pan, as shown in Figure B. Place the pie pan on top of the stove to cool. Compare the appearance of the buttons and pieces of HDPE. Do not touch the plastic pieces or buttons until they have cooled, which should take about 15 minutes.

You should find that the buttons are not changed by heating. However, the triangular pieces of HDPE should melt and change shape. The melted plastic tends to flow onto the pie pan before it cools.

Why is the behavior of the plastic buttons and the other pieces of plastic so different? Buttons and HDPE pieces represent two completely different types of plastic, called *thermoplastics* and *thermosets*. These types of plastic differ in the way they are affected by heating. High-density polyethylene is a thermoplastic material. Buttons are usually made of thermoset material.

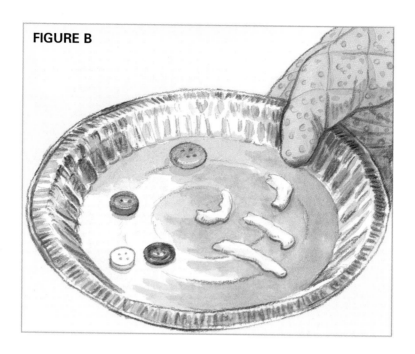

FIGURE B

Thermoplastics such as polyethylene soften and flow at high temperatures. When they reach a high enough temperature, they become elastic, like rubber. At an even higher temperature, they melt and change to a liquid. When thermoplastics are allowed to cool, they become hard again. Hot liquid thermoplastics can be poured into a mold and allowed to cool and harden into the shape of the mold.

A piece of ice, if its temperature is raised, will melt and turn into a liquid; but if it is cooled, it will change back into a solid. Just as you can melt and harden water over and over by heating and cooling, you can melt and harden thermoplastic materials. Examples of thermoplastics include polyethylene (PE) used for containers, polystyrene (PS) used for disposable cups, and polyethylene terephthalate (PETE) used for soft-drink bottles.

One advantage in using thermoplastic materials is that they can be recycled. The containers can be collected, melted by heating, and formed into new products. Codes were added to plastics to make it easier to sort them for recycling. Today there are thousands of locations in communities around the United States where plastics are collected for recycling. The most commonly recycled plastics are coded 1 for polyethylene terephthalate (PETE) and 2 for high-density polyethylene (HDPE).

Thermosets such as melamine formaldehyde, which is used to make buttons, do not soften or flow when heated. They cannot be recycled because it is not possible to melt the material to form it into a new shape. Because of the interlocking bonds between all the molecules, thermoset polymers are locked into a rigid three-dimensional shape that cannot be changed. Even at a very high temperature, the structure of the thermoset would be destroyed before it would melt to form a liquid.

Glass-reinforced polyester (GRP) is another example of a thermoset. GRP is strong material that can be formed into curved pieces. Because it is extremely strong and resists changes due to heat or chemicals, GRP is used in automobile body parts and boat hulls.

One of the earliest commercially successful plastics (patented in 1909 by Leo H. Baekeland) was a thermoset called Bakelite, which was made from phenol and formaldehyde. Today thermosets are often used to make hard plastic cases for objects such as radios and telephones. Can you think of new uses for plastics?

12

BREAKING DOWN A POLYMER

MATTER

LIGHT

MATERIALS NEEDED

Marking pen

Two balloons

Dark closet

Small piece of wood

Stapler

Scissors

Use a marking pen to write the letter *O* ("outside") on one of the balloons and the letter *I* ("inside") on the other balloon. Blow up both balloons, and tie each balloon closed by knotting it. The inflated balloons should be about the same size.

Place the balloon labeled I in a dark closet where it will not be disturbed. Fasten the balloon labeled O onto a small board by stapling the tied end of the balloon onto the board, as shown in Figure A. Make sure not to puncture the balloon when you staple it.

Place the board with the attached balloon outdoors. Choose a spot where it will not be disturbed and where it will be exposed to the sun during most of the day.

After three days, carefully remove the balloon labeled O from the board by lifting up on the staple. Get the balloon labeled I from the closet. Deflate both balloons by carefully cutting their knots with scissors. Once they are deflated, cut both balloons lengthwise, starting at the openings you created when you deflated them.

Stretch the balloon labeled O. Continue to stretch it several

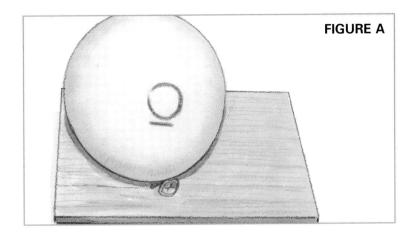

times. Next, stretch the balloon labeled I. How are the balloons different?

When you stretch the balloon labeled O, you should observe that it is less elastic than it was and that it tears or breaks easily. On the other hand, when you stretch the balloon labeled I, it is still elastic and does not tear.

Most balloons are made of natural rubber. Natural rubber is a polymer made by joining into long chains thousands and thousands of smaller molecules known as *isoprene molecules*. The long polymer chains of isoprene molecules coil and twist around each other like cooked spaghetti.

Rubber is an elastic material. An elastic material is one that returns to its original shape after it has been stretched, or deformed. Rubber is elastic because the polymer chains in rubber are coiled like a spring and because the coiled polymer chains are cross-linked together. Cross-linked polymers have bonds linking adjacent polymer chains together. In rubber, sulfur atoms cross-link the polymer chains. The process of cross-linking rubber, called *vulcanization*, was discovered by Charles Goodyear in 1839.

Cross-linked rubber molecules are still free to uncoil and stretch. The cross-links pull the chains of rubber molecules back to their original shape, as shown in Figure B. Rubber bands and

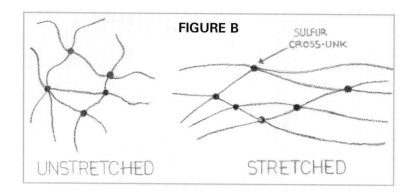

FIGURE B

SULFUR CROSS-LINK

UNSTRETCHED   STRETCHED

balloons snap back when stretched because the rubber molecules in them are cross-linked.

The rubber from the balloon left outside has lost elasticity and tears easily because sunlight and oxygen have caused some of the rubber molecules to break down by a process called *oxidation*. The oxidation of rubber molecules causes the large rubber molecules to break down into smaller molecules. Oxidation can also break the cross-links between coiled polymer chains in the rubber. The breakdown of large rubber molecules and the breaking of cross-links between rubber molecules decreases the strength of the rubber and thus makes it less elastic.

Although the balloon that was kept in the dark closet was exposed to oxygen in the air, it was not exposed to oxygen in the presence of sunlight. The rubber from this balloon remains elastic and does not tear easily because it was not exposed to strong oxidation conditions like the balloon kept outdoors.

Like natural rubber, most polymers will oxidize if left outdoors. For that reason, nearly all polymers that are made to be used outdoors contain stabilizers that help keep the polymers from breaking down by oxidation. For example, the polymer used to make car tires, a synthetic rubber called *SBR rubber*, contains stabilizers that not only retard oxidation but also retard the breakdown of the polymer by pollutants such as ozone.

13

CHANGING THE SHAPE OF PLASTIC

HEAT

MATTER

MATERIALS NEEDED

Lid or other piece of
   clear plastic with the
   code *4, LDPE*

Scissors

Ruler

Aluminum pie pan

Quarter

Oven

Oven mitt or pot
   holder

Clock or watch

❗ **Alert! Adult supervision needed.**

Can the shape of plastic be changed? In this activity you will try to mold an image into a piece of plastic.

Find a plastic lid, such as a coffee-can lid, that has the letters *LDPE* and a code number 4 inside a triangle. This number and letter code are used to indicate that the plastic material is made of low-density polyethylene.

Cut a 2-in. (5-cm) square along each side, out of the LDPE plastic. Place it on an aluminum pie pan. Set a quarter face down on top of this square piece of plastic.

Turn the oven temperature to 300°F (149°C), and wait 20 minutes for the oven to become hot. Use an insulated oven mitt to hold the aluminum pie pan and carefully place it on a rack in the oven, as shown in Figure A. Be sure that the quarter is still on top of the piece of plastic in the pie pan.

Close the oven door, and wait 8 minutes while the plastic

FIGURE A

becomes warm. After 8 minutes turn off the oven, and use the oven mitt to carefully remove the pie pan. Set the pie pan on top of the stove to cool. After about 10 minutes, when the plastic is no longer warm, peel the quarter off the plastic. Hold up the piece of plastic so you can look through it. What do you see?

You will probably see the image of George Washington's face molded into the piece of plastic. If you do not see anything in the plastic, or if the image is not clear, repeat the experiment, but change the length of time the coin and plastic are in the oven or change the temperature setting of the oven. **Do not leave the plastic in the oven for more than 12 minutes. Do not set the oven higher than 350°F (177°C)**.

When you heat the LDPE in the oven, the plastic softens and the weight of the quarter on top pushes down on the plastic. As the plastic becomes softer and more like a liquid, it molds itself to exactly fit the surface of the quarter. When the plastic cools and hardens and the quarter is removed, the image of George Washington on the face of the quarter is molded into the plastic.

Even though the heated polymer is not completely converted to a liquid, it has properties like both a solid and a liquid. It will flow slowly, and its shape can be changed. When the temperature is lower, the polymer will hold its shape. Some polymers, called *thermoplastics*, can be heated and molded over and over.

Low-density polyethylene is a thermoplastic that can be heated and softened and cooled and hardened many times. Two of the methods used to mold or shape thermoplastics are discussed below.

In *extrusion molding*, granules of plastic are heated and pushed through a hole in a heated piece of metal. Extrusion is used for making fiber filaments, pipes, and sheets of thin film. The shape formed depends on the shape of the opening through which the plastic is forced. As the warm plastic exits the heated metal, it is cooled by water, air, or metal rollers.

In *injection molding*, plastic is heated and forced into a cold metal mold by a turning screw that acts like a ram. The plastic cools in the shape of the mold. In another type of injection molding, called *blow molding*, warm, soft plastic is placed in the mold. Compressed air is blown into the mold until the plastic expands to fill the mold. This method can be used to make bottles or other hollow containers.

A LONGER RUBBER BAND

MATTER

Can you permanently change the length of a polymer by stretching it? In this experiment you will find out what happens to the length of a rubber band after it has been stretched for several days.

Lay the rubber band down alongside a ruler, as shown in Figure A. Make sure the rubber band is flat, but do not pull on the band to stretch it out. Measure the distance from one end of the band to the other. On a piece of notebook paper, write down the date, the time, and the length of the unstretched rubber band.

Stretch the rubber band around the bottom of a wastebasket that is about 40 in. (102 cm) in *circumference* (length around). This will stretch the rubber band to about five times its unstretched length. Leave the rubber band in the stretched position for about 24 hours.

The next day, remove the stretched rubber band. Measure the rubber band's unstretched length as you did the previous day. Write down the date, the time, and the length.

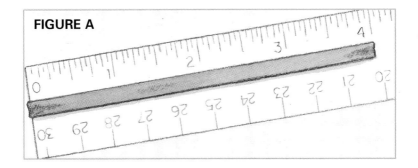

FIGURE A

Again, stretch the rubber band around the wastebasket and leave it overnight. Remove the rubber band the next day, and measure and record the length as you did previously. Compare the length of the rubber band on each day.

When you stretch a rubber band, it gets longer. When you release a stretched rubber band, you may expect it to return to its earlier unstretched length. However, in this experiment you probably found that the rubber band remained slightly longer after it had been stretched overnight. The rubber band did not return to its original unstretched length. Leaving the rubber band stretched for a second day may cause it to lengthen even more. You should find that the rubber band is several centimeters longer than its original length after being stretched for a couple of days.

Leave the rubber band unstretched and measure its length each day for several days. Does the rubber band gradually return to its original, shorter length?

Rubber bands are made of styrene-butadiene rubber (SBR) or *polyisoprene* (natural rubber). The long chains in either SBR or natural rubber must be linked together with sulfur atoms to make a useful rubber band. It is these cross-links between the long chains that cause a rubber band to *contract* (snap back into position) after it is stretched.

In an unstretched rubber band, the polymer chains are coiled together in a small space like long, wet spaghetti strands tangled together. If you pull on the ends of these strands, you can imagine them becoming many times longer than when they were coiled together. In the same way, when you stretch a rubber band, the long polymer chains become many times longer than when they were coiled closely together.

A stretched wet spaghetti strand will not return to its original coiled shape. In the same way, natural rubber that does not have sulfur cross-links will not return to a shorter length. Natural rubber that is not cross-linked does not make a good rubber band because after being stretched, it does not snap back into position. As shown in Figure B, the sulfur atoms that link the chains together ensure that the chains cannot be pulled completely straight but will remain linked and will pull back together.

When a rubber band is left stretched for many hours, it does not immediately return to its unstretched, short length. If you leave the rubber band unstretched for several days, it may gradually shorten, but it will probably not return to its original length. Molecules that have had time to set in their new extended positions only slowly return to contracted positions. In addition, if cross-links have been broken, the collection of polymer molecules will never return to their original length.

Natural rubber comes from rubber trees. When these trees

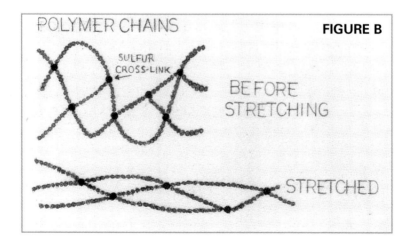

are cut, water and particles of rubber come out of the trees. This natural rubber is elastic, water-repellent, and very sticky.

The process of linking chains of rubber molecules together with sulfur, called *vulcanization*, was discovered by Charles Goodyear in 1839 after ten years of work. Vulcanization (heating with sulfur) eliminates the stickiness of natural rubber and cross-links the rubber molecules, making the rubber springy. This springy rubber goes back to its original shape after it is stretched.

In World War II, American sources of natural rubber from Asia were cut off by Japan. How would tires be made for jeeps and trucks with no rubber? What American chemists did was develop a different type of rubber, one made of styrene and butadiene molecules. This synthetic styrene-butadiene rubber (SBR) has properties similar to natural rubber and can be used to make tires.

In 1955, scientists at the Goodyear Company and at the Firestone Company found a way to make a synthetic rubber that was identical to natural rubber. Today, both natural rubber and synthetic rubber are used to make automobile tires. Either source of rubber must be vulcanized to make it cross-linked.

15

BENDING COLD POLYMERS

MATERIALS NEEDED

Plastic coffee-can lid

Refrigerator freezer

Can temperature affect the stiffness and flexibility of polymers? In this experiment you will explore what happens to the flexibility of one type of plastic as it gets colder.

Use a plastic lid from a coffee can or other similar container. Hold on to each side of the plastic lid and flex or bend it up and down. Do this several times, and remember how hard or easy the plastic is to bend.

Place the plastic lid in the refrigerator freezer, and leave it there for at least 1 hour. Remove the lid and immediately try to bend it up and down just as you did earlier. Is the plastic lid easier or harder to bend? The lid will quickly warm up to the temperature of the room. After the lid warms up, try bending it again.

You will probably find that the plastic lid is easier to bend when it is at room temperature. At the colder temperature, the lid is stiffer and less flexible than when it was warm.

Plastic container lids are usually made of a type of polymer called polyethylene. These polymer molecules are made of long chains of carbon atoms linked together with 2 hydrogen atoms attached to each carbon. The molecules of polyethylene in the lid are able to move past each other when they are at room temperature. However, as the temperature is lowered, the collection of molecules becomes more rigid and locked into position.

Within the polyethylene are regions where molecules are lined up next to each other. These regions are called *crystalline regions*. Other regions where the molecules do not line up very well are random ones and are called *amorphous regions*. (See Figure A.) The molecules are held more strongly together when they are lined up next to each other. As the temperature is lowered, there is less energy for the molecules to move past each other, and the attractions between nearby chains of polymer molecules become stronger. This change makes the plastic stiffer and more difficult to bend.

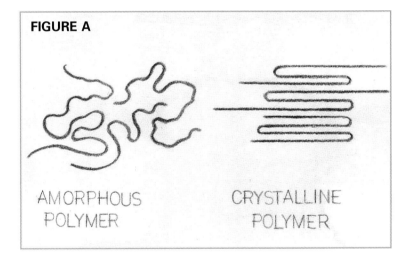

FIGURE A

AMORPHOUS POLYMER

CRYSTALLINE POLYMER

If you had a collection of tangled tree branches, you could easily bend the branches. However, if you had a series of sticks neatly stacked together, it would be very difficult to bend the sticks. The tangled tree branches are like the random (amorphous) regions of the polyethylene, and the stacked sticks are like the organized (crystalline) regions of the polyethylene.

There is a temperature called the *glass transition temperature* above which a polymer is flexible and below which a polymer is extremely rigid. However, even above the glass transition temperature, the polymer may become stiffer as the temperature is lowered.

On January 28, 1986, the space shuttle *Challenger* exploded shortly after launch and killed all seven astronauts on board. It was later discovered that a rubber ring used to seal in hot gases had failed and allowed burning gas to escape. This escaping hot gas from the solid rocket booster ignited the main hydrogen fuel tank and caused the explosion. The launch took place on an unusually cold Florida morning, and the rubber ring failed to seal in the gas because the cold temperature made the rubber polymer stiffer and less flexible.

Understanding even simple properties of matter is extremely important in engineering and construction. Can you think of engineering applications where it is essential to understand the basic properties of matter?

16

BOUNCING BALLS

MATTER   ENERGY

MATERIALS NEEDED

Two identical tennis
balls

Refrigerator freezer

Can temperature affect the bounce of something made of a polymer? In this experiment you will determine how the bouncing height of a ball is affected by temperature.

Use two identical tennis balls. Hold both balls in front of you, and drop them on a hard surface. They should bounce to the same height. If they don't, then try another pair of tennis balls.

After you have shown that the balls have the same bouncing height, place one of the balls in a refrigerator freezer. Wait 3 hours to allow the ball in the freezer to become cold. Remove the cold ball from the freezer. Hold both balls directly in front of you, and drop them on a hard surface, as shown in Figure A. You may want to drop the balls several time to repeat the experiment.

Do the balls bounce to the same height? If not, which ball bounces higher?

You should find that the warmer ball bounces higher than the cold ball. However, if you allow the colder ball to warm up to room temperature, you should find that both balls again bounce to the same height. You can repeat this experiment using different types of solid rubber balls. However, the results can vary because the type of rubber from which the balls are made varies.

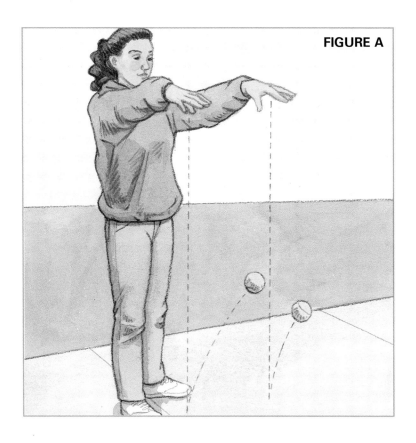

Polymer molecules in a rubber ball are arranged in a random way, with some empty space between the long polymer chains. When a rubber ball is dropped and strikes the floor, the polymer chains are pushed closer together, as shown in Figure B. Like a compressed spring, the polymer chains push apart to return to their original, uncompressed shape. As the polymer molecules push apart from each other, the ball bounces off the floor.

When the temperature of the ball is lowered, the polymer chains become stiffer and lock into position. A cold ball has a weaker bounce than a warm ball because the polymer molecules are less able to be compressed together. The gas inside the ball may also affect the bounce.

When a metal ball, such as a ball bearing, is dropped, it will

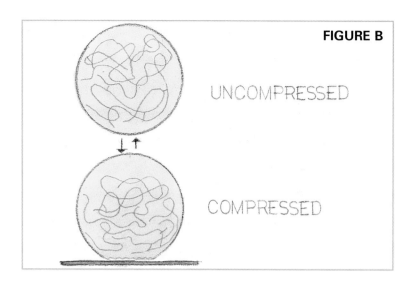

FIGURE B

UNCOMPRESSED

COMPRESSED

not bounce nearly as high as a rubber ball. The metal atoms are already packed close together and cannot easily be pushed closer. When a metal ball strikes the floor, most of the energy of falling is converted to sound and heat rather than bouncing. Try dropping a solid metal coin or a metal ball bearing on a hard surface. Does the metal object sound louder and bounce less than a rubber ball dropped from the same height?

Different types of rubber molecules behave differently when dropped on a hard surface. Rubber balls, which return rapidly to their original shape, will bounce higher than balls that return slowly to their original shape. In a racquet ball or tennis ball, where a strong bounce is important, it is necessary to use a polymer that returns quickly to its original shape. On the other hand, you do not want a bouncy rubber polymer in a running shoe because all the impact energy would be passed on to the runner's foot and leg. Rather, you want a shoe that is spongier and will absorb most of the energy of impact.

SCIENCE CONCEPTS

CONCEPT	PAGES
	9, 12, 14, 17, 20, 23, 27, 30, 40, 44, 47, 50, 54, 57
	33, 36, 54, 57
	23, 27, 44
	20, 33, 36, 40, 47, 54

FURTHER READING

To explore further the properties of plastics and polymers:

Cooper, Christopher. *Matter.* New York: Dorling Kindersley, 1992.

Darling, David. *From Glasses to Gases: The Science of Matter.* New York: Dillon Press, 1992.

Mebane, Robert C., and Thomas R. Rybolt. *Adventures with Atoms and Molecules: Chemistry Experiments for Young People.* 4 vols. Hillside, N.J.: Enslow, 1985–1992.

Newton, David. *Consumer Chemistry Projects for Young Scientists.* New York: Franklin Watts, 1991.

_____. *Science–Technology–Society Projects for Young Scientists.* New York: Franklin Watts, 1991.

Peacock, Graham, and Cally Chambers. *The Super Science Book of Materials.* New York: Thomson Learning, 1993.

Rainis, Kenneth G. *Environmental Science Projects for Young Scientists.* New York: Franklin Watts, 1994.

VanCleave, Janice. *Janice VanCleave's Chemistry for Every Kid.* New York: Wiley, 1989.

Whyman, Kathryn. *Plastics.* New York: Franklin Watts, 1988.*

* No longer in print, but you may be able to find a copy in your school or public library.

INDEX

amorphous regions, 16, 55

Baekeland, Leo H., 43
blow molding, 49

carbon atoms, 21, 54
carbon, 18, 19, 21, 22, 54
cellulose, 10, 12, 13, 29
Challenger, 56
chemical energy, 37, 38
cotton, 9–12, 29
cross-linking, 45, 46
crystalline regions, 16, 55

Dacron, 10
deflected light, 29
diapers, 13
double-pane window, 35
Dow Chemical Company, 34

E. I. Du Pont de Nemours, 21
elastic, 42, 45, 46, 53
ethylene molecules, 15, 16, 25, 31
extrusion molding, 49

fabrics, 9, 11
Firestone Company, 53

fluorine atom, 22
food chain, 38
formaldehyde, 43

gas, 31, 32, 34, 35, 56, 58
gasoline, 37
glass-reinforced polyester (GRP), 43
glass transition temperature, 55, 56
glucose, 10, 28, 29
Goodyear, Charles, 45, 53
Goodyear Company, 53
granules, 29, 49

heat, 20, 27, 31, 33–39, 41, 43, 49, 59
high-density polyethylene, 14–16, 40, 41, 43
hydrogen, 18, 19, 21, 54, 56
hydrophilic polymers, 10
hydrophobic polymers, 11

I. G. Farbenindustrie, 34
injection molding, 49
isoprene molecules, 45

latex polymer, 29
light, 23–26, 29, 37

light rays, 23
linen, 10, 29
low-density polyethylene, 14–16, 47, 49

mechanical energy, 37, 38
melamine formaldehyde, 43
muscles, 37

natural fibers, 10, 29
natural rubber, 45, 46, 51–53
nonpolar molecules, 11

oxidation, 46
oxygen, 18, 46

pentane, 34
permeability, 32
petroleum, 11
photosynthesis, 10, 28, 38
pigments, 29
plants, 10, 12, 28, 29, 38
polarized light, 23, 25, 26
polar molecules, 10, 11
polyester, 9–11, 43
polyethylene (PE), 14–16, 21, 25, 31, 32, 40–43, 47, 49, 54, 55
polyethylene terephthalate (PETE), 42, 43

polyisoprene, 51
polymerization, 16
polystyrene (PS), 33–35, 42
polytetrafluoroethylene (PTFE), 21

recycling, 43
relaxed state, 25
rubber, 32, 42, 45, 46, 50–53, 56–59

silicone polymer, 18, 19
Silly Putty, 17–19
solar energy, 38
sound energy, 37
styrene-butadiene rubber (SBR), 46, 51, 53
Styrofoam, 33–35
sugar, 10, 28

Teflon, 20–22
thermoplastic, 41, 42, 49
thermoset, 41, 43

vulcanization, 45, 53

water, 9–13, 27–29, 34, 36, 42, 49, 53

ABOUT THE AUTHORS

Rob Mebane teaches chemistry at the University of Tennessee at Chattanooga, where in 1990 he was a recipient of the Student Government Outstanding Teaching Award. He is the author of many articles in scientific journals and, with Tom Rybolt, has written fifteen nonfiction books for young people. Dr. Mebane lives in Chattanooga, where in his leisure time he enjoys white-water canoeing, backpacking, and cooking.

Tom Rybolt holds a doctorate in physical chemistry and is also on the faculty of the University of Tennessee at Chattanooga. He has written extensively for scientific journals, and in 1991 he was a recipient of the Student Government Outstanding Teaching Award. He lives in Chattanooga with his wife, Ann, and their four children, and enjoys reading, running, and raising children.